We will remember

By Nicola Webb

Illustrations by Itsumi Yamamoto and Nicola Webb

Dedicated to those who have fallen and those who keep fighting

~ we will remember.

We will remember

Each and every November

And in between those days too

The fallen soldiers people knew.

Today we stand and learn and stare

We look and listen and show we care,

By this cold and hard white stone

That stands in rows, not alone.

Fallen soldiers - there are hundreds more

Who lie in dirt or upon a shore

Lost at sea or beneath the sand

Some forever, in no man's land .

We remember those who fought so hard

For the peace they sought, and got so scarred

For the freedoms that our nations craved

And the futures that for us they saved.

And in this hour upon this day

We stand in silence and we pray:

That no more sons and daughters die

Nor families say a hard goodbye.

We remember these people now

Strong and brave and just how

They gave their lives for us to thrive:

It's so important for us, to live and strive.

And in this moment, I fall silent too.

I remember them, their stories, you.

The fight for peace takes yet another turn

From your legacy we have lots to learn.

This cold white grave stands tall and proud:

You lie near me beneath your earthly shroud.

I feel at peace, calm and hope renew;

Do you feel this silence too?

No more guns and smoke to fear

In this moment with you just here

On this hour and day in November.

Thank you for your life - we will remember.

Library and Archives Canada Cataloguing in Publication
CIP data on file with the National Library and Archives

ISBN paperback 978-1-55483-571-3

www.ingramcontent.com/pod-product-compliance
Lightning Source LLC
Chambersburg PA
CBHW061051090426
42740CB00002B/119